Intentionally Blank

Intentionally Blank

Intentionally Blank

Intentionally Blank

Intentionally Blank

Intentionally Blank

Intentionally Blank

Intentionally Blank

Intentionally Blank

Intentionally Blank

Intentionally Blank

Intentionally Blank

Intentionally Blank

Intentionally Blank

Intentionally Blank

Intentionally Blank

Intentionally Blank

Intentionally Blank

Intentionally Blank

Intentionally Blank

Intentionally Blank

Intentionally Blank

Intentionally Blank

Intentionally Blank

Intentionally Blank

Intentionally Blank

Intentionally Blank

Intentionally Blank

Intentionally Blank

Intentionally Blank

Intentionally Blank

Intentionally Blank

Intentionally Blank

Intentionally Blank

Intentionally Blank

Intentionally Blank

Intentionally Blank

Intentionally Blank

Intentionally Blank

Intentionally Blank

Intentionally Blank

Intentionally Blank

Intentionally Blank

Intentionally Blank

Intentionally Blank

Intentionally Blank

Intentionally Blank

Intentionally Blank

Intentionally Blank

Intentionally Blank

Intentionally Blank

Intentionally Blank

Intentionally Blank

Intentionally Blank

Intentionally Blank

Intentionally Blank

Intentionally Blank

Intentionally Blank

Intentionally Blank

Intentionally Blank

Intentionally Blank

Intentionally Blank

Intentionally Blank

Intentionally Blank

Intentionally Blank

Intentionally Blank

Intentionally Blank

www.ingramcontent.com/pod-product-compliance
Lightning Source LLC
Chambersburg PA
CBHW060001300526
45794CB00003B/1035